Kilmanns
Organizational Belief
Survey

RALPH H. KILMANN
AND ASSOCIATES

Distributed by
KILMANN DIAGNOSTICS
1 Suprema Drive
Newport Coast, CA 92657
www.kilmanndiagnostics.com
info@kilmanndiagnostics.com
949.497.8766

Introduction

This survey assesses your beliefs about what you can control in your surroundings. While many aspects of work are subject to control, this survey presents thirty basic aspects of organization life that affect job performance. After the completion of this assessment, your individual responses can be developed into organizational profiles.

Response Scale

Carefully study the response scale below. You will be asked to use the numbers on this scale to record your responses to thirty items. To ensure an accurate assessment, please keep these five numbers—and what they mean—clearly in mind while you respond to each item in this survey. You may refer back to this page at any time.

1   *I strongly disagree* with this statement. It does not at all reflect my beliefs. It is rarely, if ever, accurate about what I believe to be true.

2   *I disagree* with this statement. It is accurate in some instances, but it does not really capture what I believe to be true most of the time.

3   *I am neutral* about this statement or I am mixed: At times I would agree with it, but an equal number of times I would disagree.

4   *I agree* with this statement. It does tend to capture what I believe to be true, but it is not accurate in all instances.

5   *I strongly agree* with this statement. It fully reflects my beliefs all of the time. It is rarely inaccurate about what I believe to be true.

Instructions

On the next pages you will find thirty statements concerning whether or not you can control what goes on in your organization. Please circle the number on the scale that represents the extent to which you agree or disagree with the statement. While some items concern just your own work group or your immediate coworkers, other items consider *other* work groups, departments, or the organization as a whole. Even if these latter work units seem far removed from your daily job, you should still respond according to what you believe you can or cannot control in your organization.

ORGANIZATIONAL BELIEF SURVEY

		Disagree (1)		3		Agree (5)
1.	If necessary, I can change the work procedures in my department.	1	2	3	4	5
2.	I cannot improve my chances for promotion in my organization.	1	2	3	4	5
3.	I can decline to work overtime.	1	2	3	4	5
4.	No matter what I say, my fellow workers will do as they please.	1	2	3	4	5
5.	I can persuade my coworkers to be team players.	1	2	3	4	5
6.	I cannot change the number of management levels in my organization.	1	2	3	4	5
7.	I can persuade other departments to see things from my point of view.	1	2	3	4	5

ORGANIZATIONAL BELIEF SURVEY

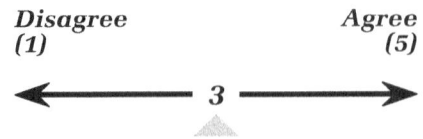

		Disagree (1)		3		Agree (5)

8. I cannot limit the amount of paper-work required by my organization.

    1   *2*   *3*   *4*   *5*

9. Management will seriously review my ideas for organizational change and improvement.

    1   *2*   *3*   *4*   *5*

10. It is unlikely that I can impress my boss with my inventiveness and creativity.

    1   *2*   *3*   *4*   *5*

11. Company policies can be shaped by nonmanagement personnel.

    1   *2*   *3*   *4*   *5*

12. I have no influence on how my organization is designed into departments and divisions.

    1   *2*   *3*   *4*   *5*

13. I can negotiate changes in my job objectives and priorities with my boss.

    1   *2*   *3*   *4*   *5*

ORGANIZATIONAL BELIEF SURVEY

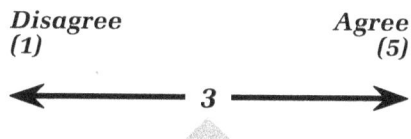

		Disagree (1)				Agree (5)

14. There is no point in trying to challenge the traditional ways of doing things in this organization.

  1   2   3   4   5

15. I can pick the people who work with me.

  1   2   3   4   5

16. I cannot influence how suppliers view my organization.

  1   2   3   4   5

17. I can talk my boss into providing more frequent reviews of my performance.

  1   2   3   4   5

18. I have little chance of motivating those at the home office to visit our other locations more frequently.

  1   2   3   4   5

19. I can promote cooperation within my department.

  1   2   3   4   5

	Disagree (1)		3		Agree (5)

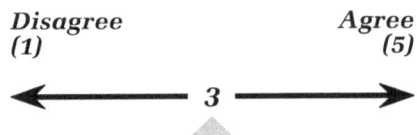

20. No matter what decisions have been made in group meetings, people will subsequently pursue their own agendas.

    1   2   3   4   5

21. If I need additional education or training, I can get it.

    1   2   3   4   5

22. I have little hope of modifying the organization-wide performance appraisal system.

    1   2   3   4   5

23. If necessary, I have the power to refocus my organization's strategic mission.

    1   2   3   4   5

24. I cannot induce the "powers that be" to change our organization's benefits program.

    1   2   3   4   5

25. I can prevail upon my boss to change my job description and classification when warranted.

    1   2   3   4   5

	Disagree (1)		3		Agree (5)
26. I cannot get the resources I need to do my job effectively.	1	2	3	4	5
27. I can influence how customers view our organization.	1	2	3	4	5
28. I cannot do much to improve the overall reputation of my organization.	1	2	3	4	5
29. I can get the information I need by asking the right people.	1	2	3	4	5
30. I have a hard time inspiring my coworkers to do their very best.	1	2	3	4	5

Scoring Your Responses

In the spaces next to the items on the following page, please transfer the numbers you circled on the previous pages of this survey. You will find it easiest to transfer your responses in sequence from item 1 through 30. It is essential that you transfer every number accurately.

Next, please add up each of the two columns. Then, as shown, subtract the sum for Column Two from the sum for Column One to obtain "My Control Score." Make sure to show a minus sign (–) on your score if the sum for Column Two on the right is larger than the sum for Column One on the left (for example: 30 – 45 = –15). Otherwise show a plus sign (for example: 40 – 25 = +15).

ORGANIZATIONAL BELIEF SURVEY

1. _____   2. _____

3. _____   4. _____

5. _____   6. _____

7. _____   8. _____

9. _____   10. _____

11. _____   12. _____

13. _____   14. _____

15. _____   16. _____

17. _____   18. _____

19. _____   20. _____

21. _____   22. _____

23. _____   24. _____

25. _____   26. _____

27. _____   28. _____

29. _____   30. _____

Sum: Column One	**Sum: Column Two**	**My Control Score**

— =

Calculating Average Control Scores

When everyone in your work group has calculated their control scores, collect all these numbers together on a separate sheet of paper and then calculate the average score for your work group. While computing this average, be sure to include the proper signs of the control scores (+ or −). Also, make certain to divide the sum of the scores by the right number of people in your group: those who actually provided their scores for this calculation.

Once the average control score has been calculated for your work group, please enter the result (with the proper sign) in the designated space on the following page for **My Work Group**. Then, if you have access to the other work groups in your department, you can also calculate the average for **My Department**. And if you have access to all the departments in your organization, you can calculate the average for **My Organization**. For your convenience, space is provided to record these latter averages (as well as your own score) including room to enter the number of respondents (N) included in the analysis. *Note:* You might find it necessary to weight the averages of each work unit by the number of its members to adjust for different sizes of groups and departments in your organization.

My Control Score	My Work Group N = ____
My Department N = ____	My Organization N = ____

Developing Organizational Belief Profiles

In each of the quadrants on the opposite page, you will see three circles of different sizes: The *outside* circle is labeled "External" and includes scores that range from −60 to −11. The *inside* circle is labeled "Internal" and includes scores that range from +11 to +60. And the *middle* circle is labeled "Mixed" and includes the scores from −10 to +10.

Please transfer your own score on the survey to the quadrant: **Individual Profile**. Shade that section of the overlapping circles that corresponds to your score. If you have calculated an average score for your work group, department, or organization, transfer the score to its appropriate quadrant and then shade its corresponding circle.

In sum, there are three different profiles that can be obtained in each of the quadrants on the opposite page—by shading one section of the three overlapping circles as follows:

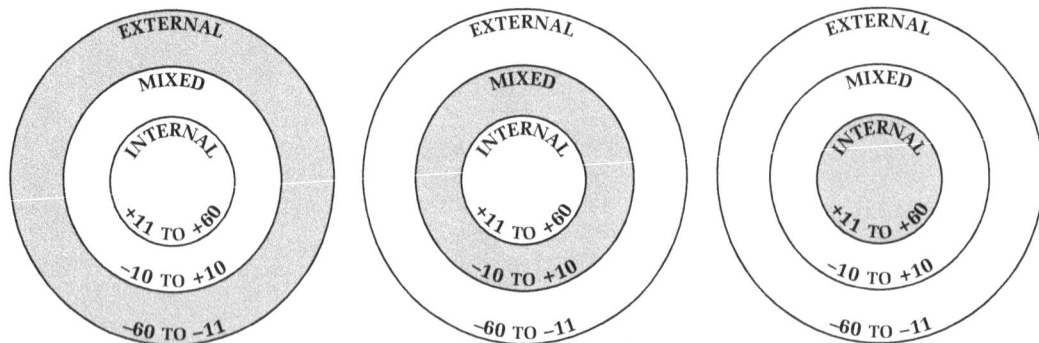

ORGANIZATIONAL BELIEF SURVEY

Individual Profile

_____

Work Group Profile

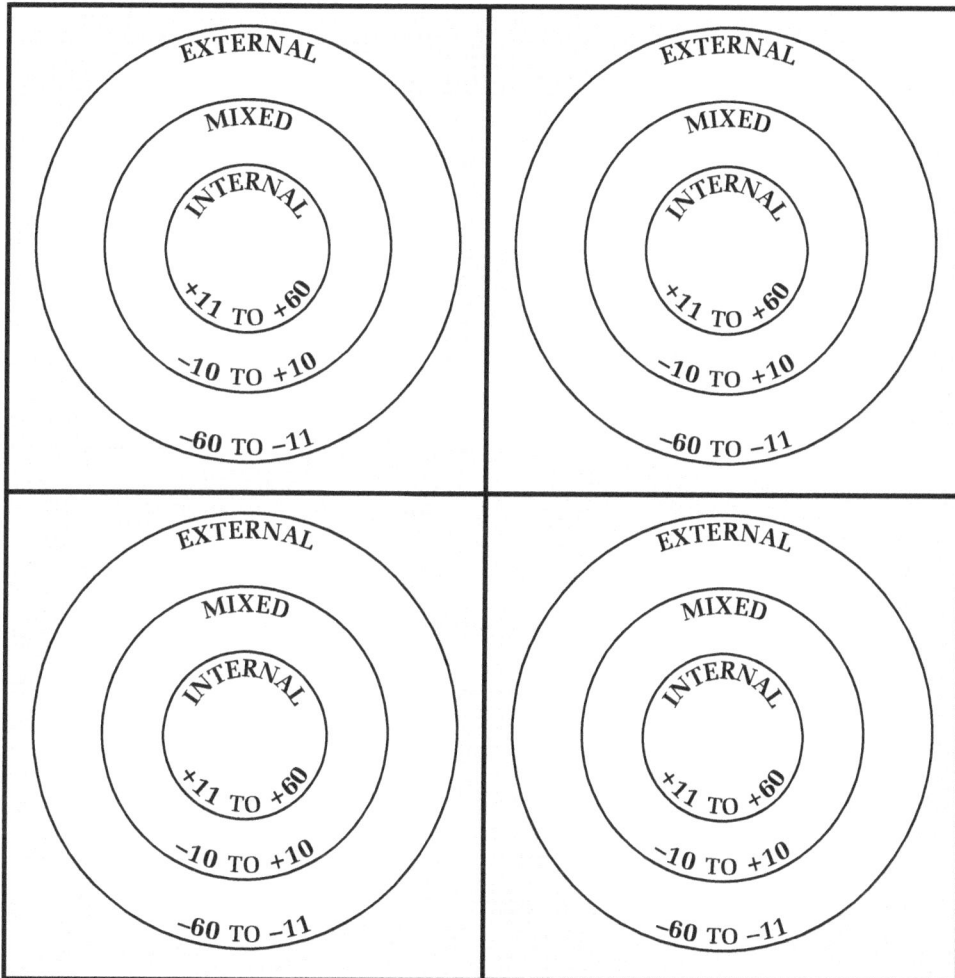

_____

EXTERNAL

MIXED

INTERNAL

+11 TO +60

−10 TO +10

−60 TO −11

EXTERNAL

MIXED

INTERNAL

+11 TO +60

−10 TO +10

−60 TO −11

EXTERNAL

MIXED

INTERNAL

+11 TO +60

−10 TO +10

−60 TO −11

EXTERNAL

MIXED

INTERNAL

+11 TO +60

−10 TO +10

−60 TO −11

Department Profile

_____

Organization Profile

_____

Defining Three Organizational Beliefs

This survey assesses whether you believe you can control the key aspects of your organization that affect your performance. For convenience sake, your score can be sorted into one of three categories: External Control, Internal Control, and Mixed Control (which match the three circles in the Organizational Belief Profiles).

Individual scores (and organizational averages) can range between –60 and +60. Recall: The rule of thumb for categorizing the results of this survey is as follows:

External Control	Mixed Control	Internal Control
–60 to –11	–10 to +10	+11 to +60

External Control means you believe that most of what goes on in your organization is determined by *outside* forces: your coworkers, your boss, your work group, your department, your organization, or people outside your organization (such as customers and suppliers). **Internal Control** means you believe that most of what goes on in your organization is determined by *inside* forces: your own attitudes, decisions, actions, and efforts to influence your surroundings. **Mixed Control**, in between these two extremes, means you believe that sometimes you can control what goes on, while at other times you cannot influence much at all.

In some situations, people's beliefs are—exactly—in line with reality: They believe they cannot influence what goes on and, indeed, they can't. Any of their attempts at change or improvement are continuously stymied by insurmountable barriers. In other situations, however, people's beliefs are considerably out of line with reality. For example, it may indeed be possible for organizational members to influence what goes on—but because they do not believe they can succeed, they do not even test their beliefs and give it a chance. Worse still is the case in which an organization gives its members an opportunity to improve performance and morale: Yet members do not *want* to believe they could make a real difference, so they *refuse* to try.

It is very difficult to know for sure which of these three scenarios is true in an organization: whether (1) beliefs are in line with reality—because members cannot improve their performance no matter how hard they try, (2) beliefs are *unknowingly* out of line—because they have not been tested recently, or (3) beliefs are *knowingly* out of line—because people *prefer,* quite intentionally, not to be responsible or accountable for their own behavior.

If an organization showed little interest in attempting to improve itself, perhaps the first scenario would be plausible. But when an organization is proceeding to implement a systemwide program of planned change, it is hard to argue that real improvement cannot take place. In this case, ironically, *the one thing that can hold the organization back is its own members' outdated and self-serving beliefs.*

Interpreting Organizational Belief Profiles

When work group, department, and organizational averages have been calculated and graphed, it is interesting to examine the similarities and differences among the beliefs about control across these work units—as compared to individual scores.

The example on the opposite page illustrates a situation in which the individual and, to a lesser extent, the work group are both somewhat pessimistic about the prospects for influencing job performance—while, at the same time, the larger department and the organization as a whole are much more optimistic. These relative profiles might suggest that the individual and his or her work group are not seeing, believing, and thus taking advantage of what most others in the organization are able to influence—and achieve—in their working environment.

By examining these results and then discussing their many implications, however, the particular individuals will be able to rethink whether their *perceptions* of various constraints, limitations, and restrictions in the situation are actually real or largely imagined. An open, candid, and thoughtful discussion along these lines might help to align individual beliefs with reality—which is more likely to foster constructive action than continued resignation.

ORGANIZATIONAL BELIEF SURVEY

Individual Profile

−28

Work Group Profile

−20

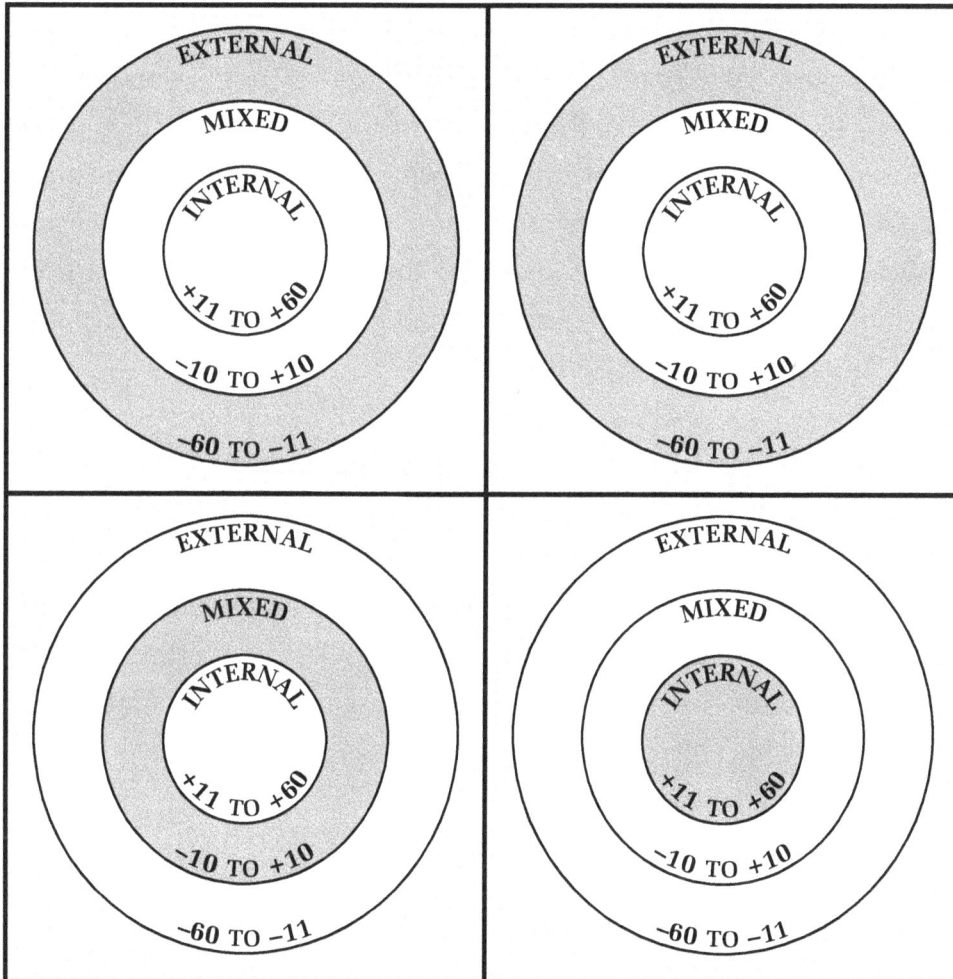

EXTERNAL MIXED INTERNAL +11 TO +60 −10 TO +10 −60 TO −11	EXTERNAL MIXED INTERNAL +11 TO +60 −10 TO +10 −60 TO −11
EXTERNAL MIXED INTERNAL +11 TO +60 −10 TO +10 −60 TO −11	EXTERNAL MIXED INTERNAL +11 TO +60 −10 TO +10 −60 TO −11

Department Profile

+7

Organization Profile

+24

Interpreting Profiles: Another Example

Now consider the four Organizational Belief Profiles shown on the next page. In this case, the individual and the work group apparently believe they *can* influence much of what determines job performance—but the department and their organization as a whole do not! Somehow, these employees have not allowed themselves to be negatively affected by the constraints and obstacles that others seem to experience (or imagine). In this case, it is not unusual for other members of the organization to say: "Hasn't anyone told them they can't do that? Don't they realize that the system will beat them down? They're acting as if they can really make a difference here and get something done!"

By making these profiles explicit, however, all members throughout the organization can be encouraged to rethink whether they are as helpless and out of control as they envision themselves to be. In particular, to discover that members and work groups *in the very same organization* have not succumbed to External Control may very well stimulate a fresh look at such beliefs—especially when the organization is making a real effort to change and improve.

ORGANIZATIONAL BELIEF SURVEY

Individual Profile

+22

Work Group Profile

+14

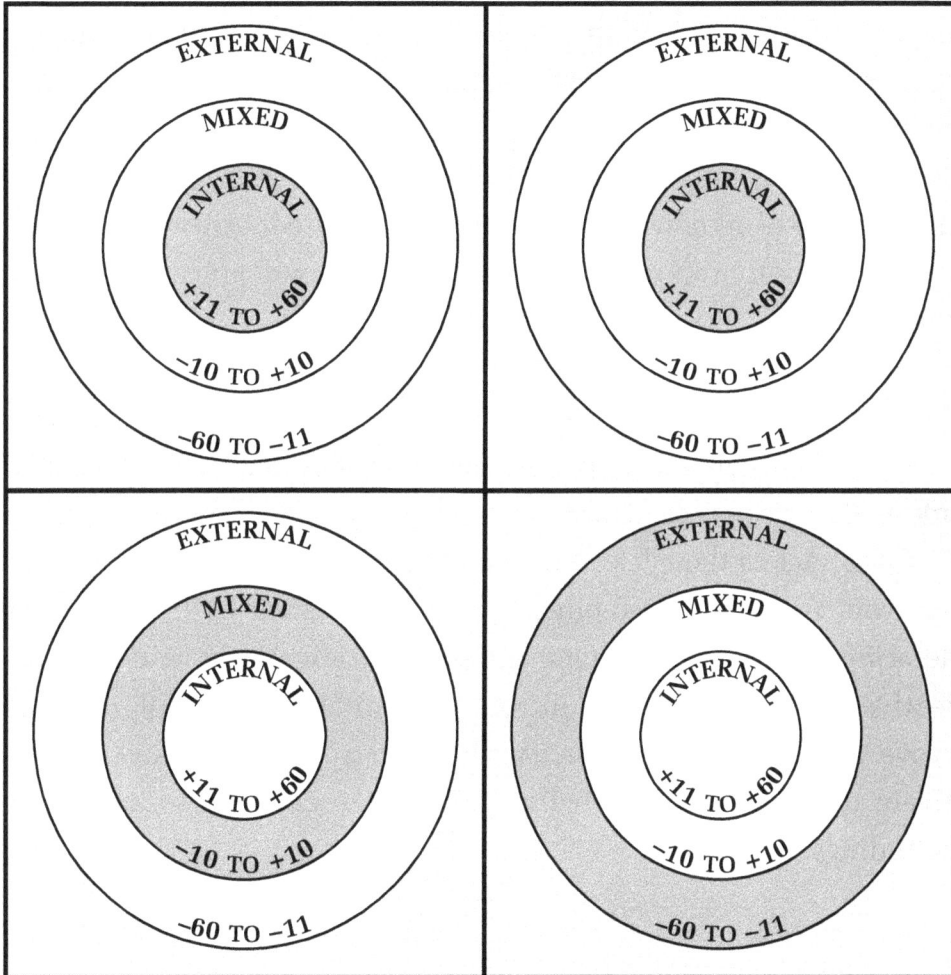

Department Profile

–5

Organization Profile

–18

The Critical Path to Internal Control

Ultimately, the challenge is to question any individual's, work group's, or department's beliefs about External Control—especially during those times when the organization is trying to improve its functioning. Even more important, a belief in Internal Control must be fostered actively in order to overcome the debilitating effects of Mixed Control—let alone External Control. Employees need to test their reality explicitly, rather than assuming—unknowingly—that they cannot control what goes on in their organization even when they are being given a sincere opportunity to do so.

To foster Internal Control, therefore, you must do the following: **See** the connection between what you do and what happens—all around you. **Think** as though you can influence what goes on in your organization—at all times. **Act** as though you can make a difference—on everything that affects you. And encourage others to believe in their ability—and will—to determine their destiny. One thing is certain: Without developing a collective belief in Internal Control, an organization cannot change and improve its performance—even with the best of intentions. You must cultivate the organizational belief that people can indeed control their surroundings!

Assessment Tools for the Eight Tracks
Distributed by Kilmann Diagnostics

Kilmann-Saxton Culture-Gap® Survey

Kilmanns Organizational Belief Survey

Kilmanns Time-Gap Survey

Kilmanns Team-Gap Survey

Organizational Courage Assessment

Kilmann-Covin Organizational Influence Survey

Plus the Online Version of the

Thomas-Kilmann Conflict Mode Instrument

9 780983 274209